Angling Series

Diseases and Parasites of Freshwater Fish

A Selection of Classic Articles on Lice, Flukes, Tapeworms and Other Fish Enemies

By

Various Authors

Copyright © 2011 Read Books Ltd.
This book is copyright and may not be
reproduced or copied in any way without
the express permission of the publisher in writing

British Library Cataloguing-in-Publication Data
A catalogue record for this book is available from
the British Library

A Short History of Fishing

Fishing, in its broadest sense – is the activity of catching fish. It is an ancient practice dating back at least 40,000 years. Since the sixteenth century fishing vessels have been able to cross oceans in pursuit of fish and since the nineteenth century it has been possible to use larger vessels and in some cases process the fish on board. Techniques for catching fish include varied methods such as hand gathering, spearing, netting, angling and trapping.

Isotopic analysis of the skeletal remains of **Tianyuan man**, a 40,000 year old modern human from eastern Asia, has shown that he regularly consumed freshwater fish. As well as this, archaeological features such as shell middens, discarded fish-bones and cave paintings show that sea foods were important for early man's survival and were consumed in significant quantities. The first civilisation to practice organised fishing was the Egyptians however, as the River Nile was so full of fish. The **Egyptians** invented various implements and methods for fishing and these are clearly illustrated in tomb scenes, drawings and papyrus documents. Simple **reed boats** served for fishing. Woven nets, weir baskets made from willow branches, harpoons and hook and line (the hooks having a length of between eight millimetres and eighteen centimetres) were all being used. By the twelfth dynasty, metal hooks with barbs were also utilised.

Despite the Egyptian's strong history of fishing, later Greek cultures rarely depicted the trade, due to its perceived low social status. There is a wine cup however, dating from c.500 BC, that shows a boy crouched on a rock with a fishing-rod in his right hand and a basket in his left. In the water below there is a rounded object of the same material with an opening on the top. This has been identified as a fish-cage used for keeping live fish, or as a fish-trap. One of the other major Grecian sources on fishing is Oppian of Corycus, who wrote a major treatise on sea fishing, the *Halieulica* or *Halieutika*, composed between 177 and 180. This is the earliest such work to have survived intact to the modern day. Oppian describes various means of fishing including the use of nets cast from boats, scoop nets held open by a hoop, spears and tridents, and various traps 'which work while their masters sleep.' Oppian's description of fishing with a 'motionless' net is also very interesting:

> *The fishers set up very light nets of buoyant flax and wheel in a circle round about while they violently strike the surface of the sea with their oars and make a din with sweeping blow of poles. At the*

> *flashing of the swift oars and the noise the fish bound in terror and rush into the bosom of the net which stands at rest, thinking it to be a shelter: foolish fishes which, frightened by a noise, enter the gates of doom. Then the fishers on either side hasten with the ropes to draw the net ashore...*

The earliest English essay on recreational fishing was published in 1496, shortly after the invention of the printing press! Unusually for the time, its author was a woman; Dame Juliana Berners, the prioress of the Benedictine Sopwell Nunnery (Hertforshire). The essay was titled *Treatyse of Fysshynge with an Angle* and was published in a larger book, forming part of a treatise on hawking, hunting and heraldry. These were major interests of the nobility, and the publisher, Wynkyn der Worde was concerned that the book should be kept from those who were not gentlemen, since their immoderation in angling might 'utterly destroye it.' The roots of recreational fishing itself go much further back however, and the earliest evidence of the fishing reel comes from a fourth century AD work entitled *Lives of Famous Mortals*.

Many credit the first recorded use of an artificial fly (fly fishing) to an even earlier source - to the Roman Claudius Aelianus near the end of the second century.

He described the practice of Macedonian anglers on the Astraeus River, '...they have planned a snare for the fish, and get the better of them by their fisherman's craft. . . . They fasten red wool round a hook, and fit on to the wool two feathers which grow under a cock's wattles, and which in colour are like wax.' Recreational fishing for sport or leisure only really took off during the sixteenth and seventeenth centuries though, and coincides with the publication of Izaak Walton's *The Compleat Angler* in 1653. This is seen as the definitive work that champions the position of the angler who loves fishing for the sake of fishing itself. More than 300 editions have since been published, demonstrating its unstoppable popularity.

Big-game fishing only started as a sport after the invention of the motorised boat. In 1898, Dr. Charles Frederick Holder, a marine biologist and early conservationist, virtually invented this sport and went on to publish many articles and books on the subject. His works were especially noted for their combination of accurate scientific detail with exciting narratives. Big-game fishing is also a recreational pastime, though requires a largely purpose built boat for the hunting of large fish such as the billfish (swordfish, marlin and sailfish), larger tunas (bluefin, yellowfin and bigeye), and sharks (mako, great white, tiger and hammerhead). Such developments have only really gained prominence in the twentieth century. The motorised boat has also meant that commercial fishing, as well as fish farming has emerged on a massive scale. Large trawling ships are common and one of the strongest markets in the world is the cod trade which fishes roughly 23,000 tons from the Northwest Atlantic, 475,000 tons from the Northeast Atlantic and 260,000 tons from the Pacific.

These truly staggering amounts show just how much fishing has changed; from its early hunter-gatherer beginnings, to a small and specialised trade in Egyptian and Grecian societies, to a gentleman's pastime in fifteenth century England right up to the present day. We hope that the reader enjoys this book, and is inspired by fishing's long and intriguing past to find out more about this truly fascinating subject. Enjoy.

Diseases and Parasites of Freshwater Fish

By H. S. Joyce

A Collection of Articles

DISEASES AND PARASITES OF FRESHWATER FISH by H. S. Joyce

THERE are, of course, many maladies to which fish, like humans, are heir, but it is not possible to discuss all of them in a series of short articles. Having covered the more general diseases and parasitic affections in my previous articles, I will end with brief mention of one or two other diseases, the frequency or seriousness of which merits their inclusion.

White Spot

White Spot is caused by a minute parasite which eats through the skin of a fish, making small pits which appear as white spots. The adult parasite, which is about one millimetre in diameter, can be seen with the naked eye moving slowly about on the victim. The young, which are quite distinct from the adults, imbed themselves in the skin of the fish and form cysts.

This disease is easy to identify by removing one of the white spots, under which, with the use of a strong pocket lens, a small roundish object containing a horseshoe-shaped nucleus will be seen. When this organism is fully formed, it falls from the fish, sinks to the bottom and attaches itself to a stone or weed, where it produces a large number of smaller free-swimming forms which in turn seek out fish to which they attach themselves.

Fish afflicted with White Spot roll about and rub themselves on the bottom in an attempt to rid themselves of their tormentors, whence the disease is sometimes referred to as the itch. If not given attention affected fish die within a few weeks. That a fish should behave in the way described must not, however, be taken as a sure indication that the disease is present. Fish quite often roll and rub themselves on the bottom when in perfect health, a procedure which sometimes indicates that they are about to feed.

In the case of pond fish suffering from White Spot, when tadpoles are available, diseased fish should be removed to a clean vessel together with a few tadpoles, which will eat the parasites. It is helpful also to place the fish in a solution of one tablespoonful of salt to each gallon of water, on alternate days, removing the fish when they show signs of distress.

White Spot is most commonly found in ponds and stagnant water; but cases have been known of heavy mortality among salmon from this disease.

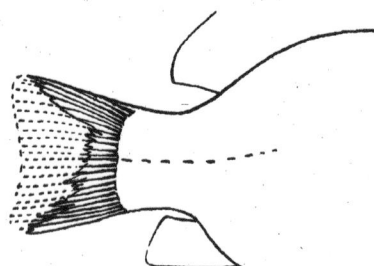

Effect of tail rot on Crucian Carp. Dots show area of erosion

Tail Rot

Tail Rot is more common in stagnant water than in running streams, and the earliest symptom is a whitish line along the edge of a tail fin. As the disease develops the fin begins to rot; but at this stage it can be cured by cutting away the diseased part and painting the remaining healthy portions with friar's balsam. If, however, tail rot reaches the base of the tail, the fish will quickly die. I have found this malady frequently among Crucian carp. It generally appears after long periods of very cold weather, particularly where the water is shallow, overstocked and thick with weeds.

Gill Disease

Gill Disease (a bacterial infection) is often very difficult to diagnose and is frequently an early stage of Saprolegnia, or fungus. The usual symptoms at its outset are dullness of the skin, refusal of the fish to feed, a desire to hide, and sometimes the appearance of whitish patches about the body. As the infection advances the gill filaments become swollen and club-shaped; the bases and sometimes the whole length of the filaments get fused together, and a considerable amount of mucus is often secreted by them. Adult fish do not as a rule seem to suffer greatly as the result of this common disease, from which they usually recover quickly if transferred to warmer water and dieted with a liberal supply of shrimps, water fleas, raw meats etc. This disease is very infectious, and young fish generally die from it if they are not segregated and given immediate treatment. Several cures are recommended, the simplest of which is to give the fish salt-water baths, using a solution of three and a half ounces of common salt to one gallon of water. The fish are left in the bath until they show signs of distress.

Gill Deformity

Gill deformity, in which there is a deficiency in the upper part of the gill covers, which in many cases exposes the upper parts of the gill's mechanism, may or may not be a disease. No one seems to know with certainty. It is, however, so regular in form that it appears to arise in almost every case from the same cause. It has been suggested that it is due to the effects of waste products from paper mills. It has also been attributed to in-breeding. I am, however, inclined to question both theories, having caught many trout and several dace and chub which exhibited this defect from waters where these causes could not be substantiated. In some cases there were paper mills on the streams from which I took the fish; in others there were none in the district. With regard to in-breeding as a cause of gill deformity, I have caught numbers of trout so afflicted from waters where restocking was so regular and opportunities for a change of blood so numerous as to discount any suggestion of it. The idea that this defect was due to in-breeding may have originated from the discovery, about 1880, that a great many trout in Malham Tarn, Yorkshire, suffered from this malformation. This tarn is certainly very isolated, and has no feeders of any size, and the outflow is absorbed by the limestone and reappears as the River Aire more than two miles distant. These circumstances, I admit, point to in-breeding being one of the causes of the defect.

It is obvious that to leave the delicate gill membranes exposed, if only slight-

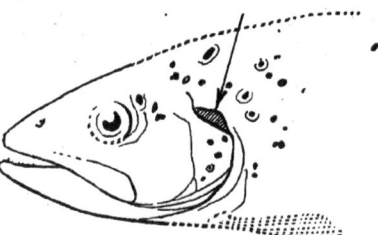

Gill deformity

ly, must render a fish susceptible to disease and injury; but all the fish I have taken with this defect have been as well-grown and healthy as others taken from the same water in which the gill covers were normal. I have sketches of a number of trout exhibiting this condition varying in extent from a small depression (as shown in the illustration above) at the upper edge of the gill covers to a large declivity over almost the whole of the top half of the cover. An interesting feature of the cases which have come to my notice is that almost exactly the same amount of defect was evident on both sides of the head.

DISEASES AND PARASITES OF FRESHWATER FISH
III—Furunculosis
by H. S. Joyce

THE destructive disease known as furunculosis first attracted attention about 1911 or 1912 when a severe outbreak occurred in some of the Devonshire rivers. Before that time it had been looked upon as a more or less occasional disease which affected salmon chiefly (other fish sometimes), and was generally referred to as "salmon disease".

The usual symptoms of this disease are the appearance of abscesses between the scales and the fish becomes sluggish and dies within a short time. Fortunately it rarely attacks fish until they have reached breeding maturity, so that waters recover in a few years from its most devastating attacks. Outbreaks are more likely to occur after severe winters, when fish are in a low state of health; but low temperatures do not encourage it. A water temperature of about 65 degrees seems to be most favourable for its development. Should the disease develop, under these conditions, deaths

Furunculosis may lurk in water as pellucid as this

will be observed within two or three weeks; but, should rain fall, thus lowering the temperature and freshening the water, an improvement will be noticed almost immediately.

Agreement has not yet been reached as to how this disease arises. The suggestion that it is always started by salmon would seem, however, to be contradicted by the appearance of furunculosis in ponds to which no salmon have access. Some authorities believe that the bacillus which causes the condition gains access to the fish through some injury; but this is disputed by others. Some assert that it is only epidemic amongst salmon and trout; but this theory cannot be relied upon.

These conflicting opinions suggest that the disease is not always correctly diagnosed. It does not necessarily follow that when a fish has abscesses on its body, it is suffering from furunculosis; but, if the abscesses, pimples or ulcers are situated mainly in the forward half of the fish, and are filled with blood-stained pus, one may be pretty certain that this is reliable evidence of the disease. An enlarged and inflamed vent, sometimes discharging, and patches of bloody-coloured flesh just under the skin are further evidence. When the disease is identified all dead and sickly fish should be removed from the water and destroyed.

In recent years little has been heard of furunculosis and hopes have been entertained that it had died out; but a few cases were reported in 1950. In one case revealed by Dr. W. Rushton, a salmon with sea lice still on it was suffering from the disease; and it is possible that it may crop up again in a serious form, when conditions are favourable.

Some contend that the bacillus which causes furunculosis lies dormant in organic matter in pools and becomes active only when fish crowd in them during droughts. But we are still apparently a long way from having all the facts, and it behoves anglers to seek remedial aid from expert quarters should an outbreak occur in their waters.

DISEASES AND PARASITES OF FRESHWATER FISH
Fish Lice

by H. S. Joyce

FISH lice belong to the family *Copepoda*, in which we find the well-known freshwater *Cyclops* and the marine *Cetochilus*, which provides a large part of the food of some whales.

Anglers in freshwater are concerned with two species: the freshwater-louse *Argullus foliaceus* and the sea-louse *Lepeophtheirus salmonis*. There are many other sea-lice, most of which bear a close superficial resemblance to *L. salmonis*, but they do not concern us here.

Freshwater-lice may be found on any freshwater fish, but I have seen them only on pike, roach and carp. They are not usually sufficiently numerous to harm the fish which they attack; and one may catch hundreds of fish without seeing a single specimen.

Sometimes, however, they appear in such numbers as to denude a pond or lake, as was the case at Lough Anasard and other near-by lakes in Co. Galway. In 1947 a friend and I fished these lakes, visiting Lough Anasard for a whole day on three occasions; but we saw no fish rise in this lough and our total bag was one nine-inch trout.

Freshwater-lice, which attach themselves to the skin of a fish by their

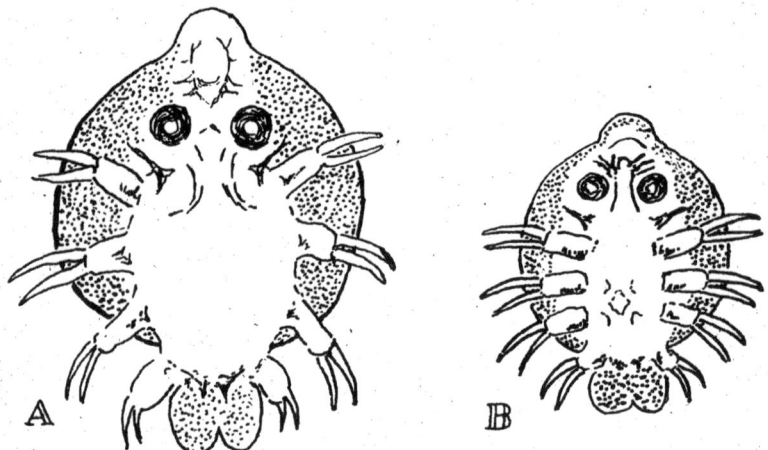

Fig. 1. Freshwater louse much enlarged. A. Female. B. Male (both ventral surface)

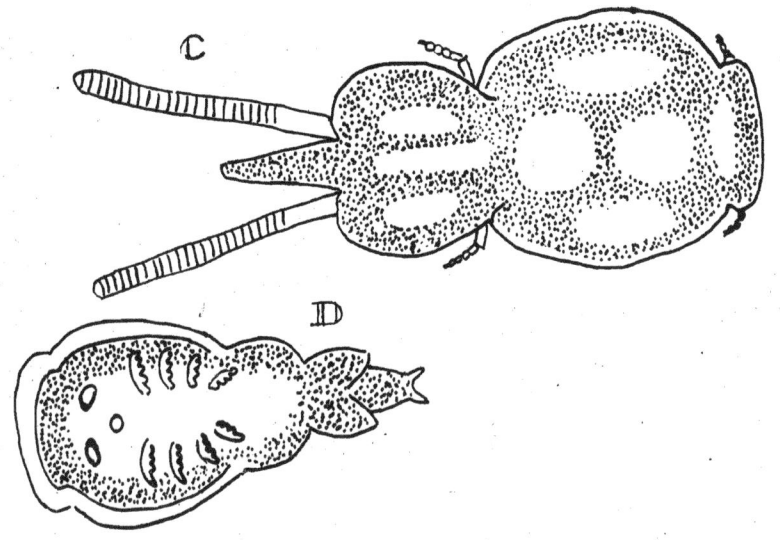

Fig. 2. Sea louse much enlarged. C. Female with eggs—dorsal surface. D. Male—ventral surface

horny carapace, which acts as a sucker, have eight legs and two eyes, but unlike the sea-louse they are tailless, Fig. 1.

Sea-lice, which are found on both salmon and sea-trout, attach themselves to their host whilst it is in salt water; and their presence is often regarded as a sure sign that the fish is fresh-run.

There does not, however, appear to be any hard and fast rule regarding the length of time during which they retain their hold. There is in fact some evidence that this may vary in different rivers. J. A. Hutton has recorded several cases of fish from the Evanger River in Norway which retained their sea-lice from fourteen to twenty-five days.

Sea-lice usually remain attached for five or six days in cold water, but fall off sooner when the water is warm. The females greatly outnumber the males of the species; the males, however, survive longer in freshwater, Fig. 2.

The female, which is larger than the male, usually sheds her eggs (which are packed in strings, on either side of the tail, very much like aspirin tablets packed in tubes) soon after entering freshwater.

When salmon have an uninterrupted run, they may be taken with sea-lice adhering many miles from the sea. In the Wye, for instance, sea-lice are frequently found on fish taken above Hereford, which is sixty miles inland.

Much remains to be learned about these creatures, but if freshwater-lice appear in large numbers, sufficient is known to warrant taking professional advice, lest their numbers become lethal.

The Editor reminds correspondents that communications requiring a reply must be accompanied by the requisite stamps, MSS will not be returned unless this condition is complied with.

DISEASES AND PARASITES OF FRESHWATER FISH
V—Flukes
by H. S. Joyce

SO many varieties of fluke attack fish that it is doubtful if there is any species which is entirely free from one or other of them. Most of these parasites which have been examined and named, up to the present time, were found on sea-fish. The fact that comparatively few have been studied in connection with freshwater fish is due probably to the fact that, in this country, freshwater fish have less commercial value and have not, therefore, attracted so much attention from scientists acting under Government control. This is not, however, the case either on the Continent or in the U.S.A. and many more flukes have been discovered on freshwater fish there.

In spite of the relatively small number of flukes that have been identified in connection with British freshwater fish, and it is with these that I am solely concerned, I should require very much more space than is now available to deal with them fully. I have, however, selected a few fairly typical examples, which are figured below, and will deal briefly with them.

Flukes, which are usually small, slug-like creatures, belong to the order *Trematoda*, a name derived from the Greek meaning a hole and referring to the suckers with which these creatures are furnished. There are two of these suckers, one at the head, the other usually about the middle of the fluke.

They do not attack fish only, by any means, and are found on mammals, birds, reptiles and even plants. There must be few living things which escape

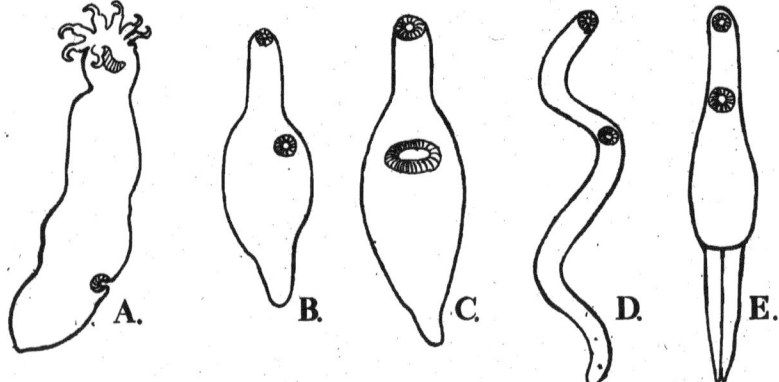

Various Flukes—A. *Bucephalus polymorphus*, B. *Podocotyle atomon*, C. *Sphaerostoma bramae*, D. *Azygia lucii*, E. *Hemiurus communis*

their attention. Some flukes live outside their hosts, others within; but in the majority of cases the victims do not seem to suffer much inconvenience unless the flukes are very numerous. Many of them are clearly visible to the naked eye and the details of nearly all can be seen easily with the aid of a hand lens. Some found on large freshwater fish may be an inch in length, but the majority are not more than one or two millimetres long.

Their life stories vary, but almost invariably each stage is passed in a different host. One might summarize the life cycle as follows.

The minute tadpole-like larva finds its way into a water snail. The snail is eaten by a fish and from this the fluke develops. The fish is then eaten by a bird and the cycle is restarted by the eggs being passed in the excrement of the bird. It follows from this rather hit-or-miss method of perpetuating the species that the eggs are produced in enormous numbers, for literally millions of them can never find the right environment for the completion of their development.

Some species of fluke are found in human beings; but not as a rule in Europeans. This is probably because we drink purer water than the peoples of other countries. We are further safeguarded by our habit of cooking most of our food.

Of the sample flukes figured, *Bucephalus polymorphus* has been found in British pike and in many other fish on the Continent. It is about one millimetre long and at one stage of its development has been found in freshwater mussels. In its early stages it is found under the skin of the fish; and when adult in the intestines.

Podocotyle atomon, which is very common around the shores of Britain in rock pools, is found in a number of sea-fish; and is included here because it is frequently identified in the intestines of eels in freshwater. This species is about three millimetres in length.

Sphaerostoma bramae has been found in roach in this country, and in perch, ruffe, pike, carp, barbel, tench, chub, minnows, dace, rudd, silver bream and loach on the Continent. It is four millimetres long and inhabits the intestines. Some authorities consider this to be one of the commonest flukes which affect British fish; but very little attention has been given to it.

Azygia lucii is one of the very few species of fluke which is worm-like in form and attains a length of from ten to thirty millimetres. They are rosy in colour when living, but fade to white when dead. They have been located in pike in Britain and in perch, burbot, trout, grayling, chub and pike in Europe. They are also present in North America. *Azygia lucii* lives in the stomach, intestines and sometimes in the gullet of its host.

Hemiurus communis is found commonly in sea-fish; and has been identified in the stomachs of eels in freshwater. It is from one to two millimetres in length and I have instanced it because it provides a variation from the more normal slug-like shape.

My diagrams are confined to the general outlines and the positions of the suckers, which are usually sufficient for purposes of identification.

PRESERVING RAGWORMS

Several readers, whether in concert or not we do not know, are anxious to obtain a reliable recipe for preserving ragworms. If there is such a recipe our researches have failed to discover it.

If you know of any really good method, please write to the Editor.

DISEASES AND PARASITES OF FRESHWATER FISH
Black Fish by H. S. Joyce

THE condition known as "Black Fish" is found chiefly among trout, but it may occur in other species. It should not, however, be confused with either the blackness of certain fish at spawning time (notably grayling and hen salmon) or with the blackness which results from living in places where very little daylight can penetrate. Trout which live in deeply wooded, rocky streams are, for example, often black fish. Trout which suffer from this supposed disease, which causes blackness, are almost invariably seen in the open and remain black, though they may be seen daily in sunny places where a normal trout would fade quickly to a scarcely-visible sandy shade.

The time was, when black fish were said to be diseased, and every endeavour was made to get them out of a water lest the disease should spread.

Later, the late Dr Mottram, propounded an ingenious theory, to the effect that this blackness was due to tar-washings. There is little doubt that he was influenced in this decision largely by his investigations in another direction. His research in connection with cancer amongst people occupied in distilling tar showed that some of the chemicals in tar were photosensitisors. It was not, therefore, surprising that he should suspect a connection with the then new practice of tarring road surfaces; and he stated that "before roads were tarred, black trout were unknown" and that "the two began simultaneously". I think he was mistaken, however. Roads were not tarred until motor cars came into general use, and, until that time, fish were many and anglers few. A plentiful supply of trout was taken for granted and a black fish or two would not cause

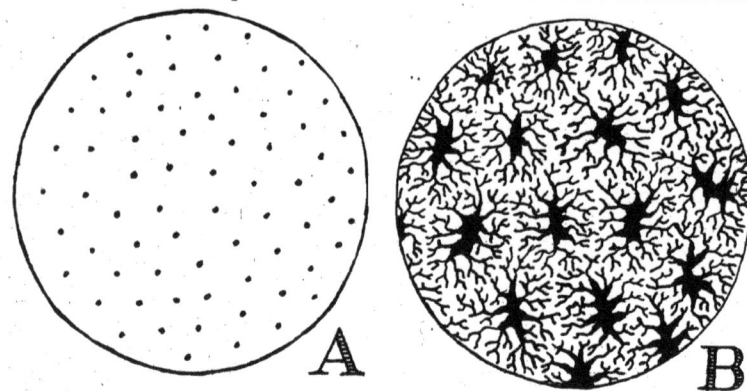

PIGMENT CELLS OF FISH
A—Cells from a light fish, showing the pigment contracted into the smallest possible space.
B—Cells of a dark fish, showing a wide distribution of the pigment

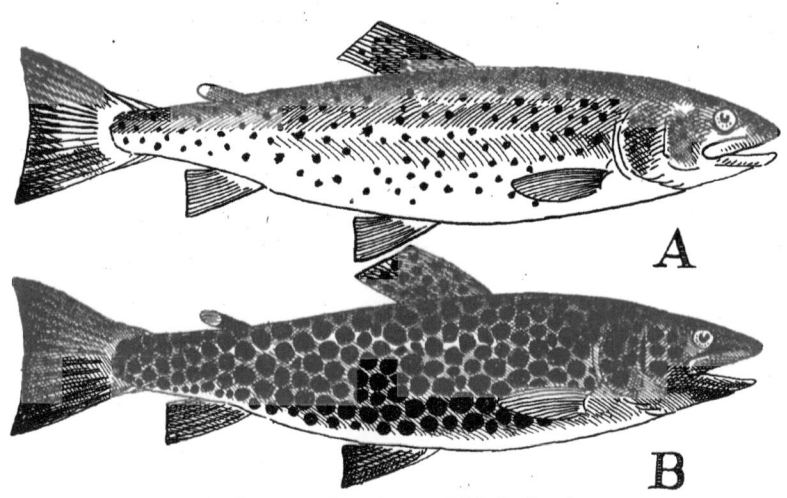

A—Sea-trout after a long period in fresh water
B—Sea-trout with greatly enlarged spots after a severe injury

much comment. Dr Mottram did, however, notice that many black trout were blind and attributed this to the same influences which caused blackness.

That very observant river keeper, F. E. Sawyer, has, however, put forward a much more likely cause of this alleged disease. He noticed that a large proportion of black fish had been wounded by herons. Nearly all such fish were either cut by herons or were blind from some cause or other. Mr Sawyer's suggestion is that the wounds and/or blindness cause a disturbance in the mechanism which enables a fish to change its colour in accordance with the amount of light which penetrates its surroundings. This mechanism operates in much the same way as do the pupils of the eyes of birds and animals, which contract or expand in response to the amount of light around them.

My own experiences support Sawyer's argument. I have caught several very black perch, all of which were deeply gashed in their backs, probably by pike. I kept a minnow for more than a year after it had been partly swallowed by a small pike. As a result it had lost all its skin from the dorsal fin to the tail fin. The tail, being skinless, remained white; but the forward half of the fish remained dark, even after the fish had been for some time in bright daylight. More convincing, however, is the case of a large sea-trout which friends and I removed from a river in Cumberland. We mistook this fish at first for a piece of waterlogged wood, but when it darted away, we not only saw that it was a fish, but that it had a terrible wound in its side. It had evidently been snatched, by either a gaff or a stroke-haul. The normal dark spots which appear on sea-trout which have been a long while in fresh water had expanded to such an extent that their outlines almost merged, and the fish look almost completely black.

Black Spot

There is a disease, known as Black

Spot, that sometimes attacks fish, which is caused by a small flattish worm of the fluke family. On their first appearance these spots are grey, they then become black and raised, and finally peel off and leave either a red mark or a sore. If one of these raised black spots is removed the worm may be seen coiled beneath it. This disease, which in common with most fish diseases, is more likely to be seen on fish in captivity, is very difficult to cure. The complaint is probably quite as frequent among wild fish, but under natural conditions it is much less likely to be noticed.

Not all black spots are due to disease, however; they may be caused by either debility, impurities in the blood, or, in the case of goldfish, by the absorption of too much nourishment through too rich a diet, a condition comparable to the fruity complexion which may result from too much alcohol. In these cases the black spots usually disappear when the excessive nourishment has been absorbed into the system.

DISEASES AND PARASITES OF FRESHWATER FISH

Tapeworms and Flatworms by H. S. Joyce

TAPEWORMS may be only a tenth of an inch in length, or several yards long. These repulsive creatures, though commonly regarded as one of the lowest forms of life, are actually among the most perfect examples of economy which it is possible to find.

Their sole purpose in life is to feed and reproduce, and, since this is so, they have divested themselves of every organ or function which is not necessary for these purposes. Since they have no need to move from one place to another, they have no limbs; and as they do not need to see, they have no eyes. On the same basis they have neither mouth, digestive system, nor excretory organs. Their waste matter is dealt with by their unfortunate host.

A tapeworm absorbs its food, which is predigested by its host, through its skin, in much the same manner as the host absorbs through the walls of its intestines such food as the tapeworm may leave. From this predigested food the creature produces a continuous chain of segments, each of which possesses both male and female elements. As these segments mature they detach themselves from the others, fertilize themselves, and then produce a vast number of spores. Some authorities regard the tapeworm as a colony composed of a number of individuals covering two generations. This view appears to depend on what are considered to be the essential features of an individual.

In most tapeworms found in fish the larva exists for a time as a free-liver, which hatches from the egg or spore as a spherical ciliated creature, and is taken in in this form, either as food or with

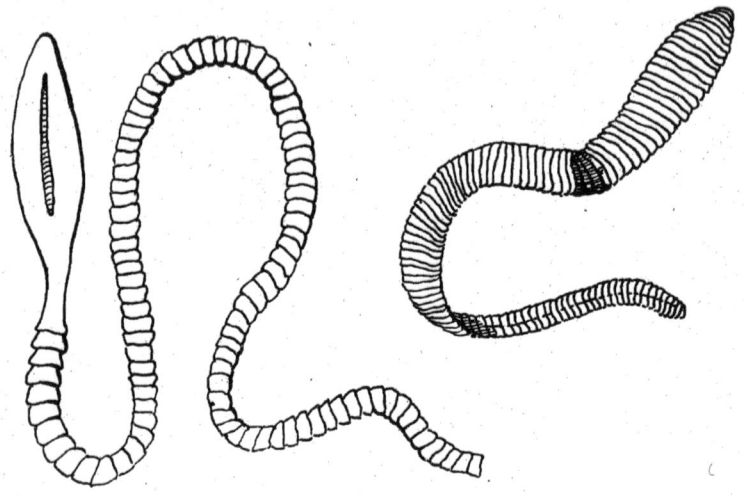

Tape worm (*Dibothriocephalus latus*), (*Right*) Flatworm

food, by its first host. The outer covering of this larva is removed, probably by mastication, and the separate central organism bores its way through the intestines into the body cavity, where it undergoes further development. The next step usally follows when the first host is devoured by a fish. The worm then enters its final stage, and, in the form of a head only, attaches itself to the intestines of its final host by means of strong hooks.

The most important tapeworm found in freshwater-fish is the broad tapeworm, *Dibothriocephalus latus*, because it can be transferred to man during the eating of raw or imperfectly cooked fish. The intermediary for this transfer is usually the pike; and human infection by this worm (which is the only fish parasite transferable to man) is quite common in the Baltic Provinces, Russia, Japan, parts of Switzerland and North America, in all of which it is customary to eat either raw or partly cooked fish.

Tapeworms do not normally appear to affect fish adversely to any great extent; though a case was recorded in 1944 (or 1945) of heavy mortality among trout which was said to have been due to the presence of these parasites.

The flatworm is an unsegmented species of tapeworm which is found in many kinds of freshwater fish, usually members of the carp family, pike and sticklebacks. I have also found it in trout and think it probable that at one time or another it must have been present in some members of every species of freshwater fish in Britain. This parasite lives within the body cavity of its host, that is to say, outside the intestines but inside the fish, though not actually in its flesh. The true tapeworm lives in the intestines; or, when in its intermediary stage, in the flesh of its host. Fish carrying a flatworm do not seem to suffer much discomfort; I have seen both roach and sticklebacks literally bulged by the large worm which they contained, but apparently in perfect health otherwise.

DISEASES AND PARASITES OF FRESHWATER FISH
Threadworms, Round or Eelworms
by H. S. Joyce

THE worms known to science as nematodes are probably the most numerous and universal of all parasites. Most of them are small, thin and white or ivory in colour, and are easily recognized by their habit of coiling and uncoiling, and twisting from side to side without progressing in any direction. They occur in the soil, in plants (doing considerable damage to root crops), in birds, animals, fish, insects, other species of nematode and man. It is the species *Trichina spiralis* which causes intestinal and muscular trichinosis, a disease which results from eating either raw or imperfectly cooked meat.

Our knowledge of the affection of fish by these parasites is very imperfect. Where they occur they are usually abundant; but from the cases which have come under my observation they do not appear to be particularly harmful provided they are not very numerous.

Some time ago I took a number of trout-carrying threadworms from a moorland reservoir. These worms were of the species *Filaria versicolor*, pinkish in colour and about two inches long. Most of them were encysted in the flesh of the fish, where they lay coiled like watch-springs; others appeared to be in the body cavity, but it is probable that these had escaped from the cysts after the death of the fish. From the outward appearance and behaviour of these fish there was nothing to indicate that they were affected, and all of them were fat and lively.

Though it is unpleasant to know that the fish you may be eating has been infested with these parasites, there is no danger to you if the fish is thoroughly cooked.

Another species of threadworm, *Cystidicola farionis*, occurs in the swim bladder of fish; generally there are only

"All of them were fat and lively"

a few, but there may be up to two hundred present. This worm looks like a small white thread; the male is about half-an-inch long and the female approximately one-and-a-half inches in length. Fish affected by these swim-bladder worms are often very dark in colour and it is fairly certain that a good many so-called black trout carry them.

Some of these worms measure only a few millimetres in length; others, such as that commonly found in pigs, may be eight inches long. Most of them produce enormous numbers of eggs: one competent biologist estimated that 60,000,000 is the probable number produced by one individual. The majority of nematodes taper at both ends, as the head is rounded and the tail pointed. Some are cylindrical throughout, and others are marked at regular intervals by fine grooves. Many are primitive in internal structure, but some have a well-developed digestive system and a number of species are hermaphrodites. It is usually accepted that the females greatly outnumber the males; but, as the males are, in most cases, very much smaller than the females, their supposed fewer numbers may be due to their being either overlooked or mistaken for young specimens.

These worms are perhaps more tenacious of life than any other living organisms. Some have been known to survive after being kept for a quarter of a century in a completely dry state. Extremes of heat and cold do not seem to affect them, for they have been found in the sands of the desert, on mountain tops and in the ice of the South Polar regions. They are sometimes present in tap water as supplied by modern and well-conducted cities, and it has been estimated that the number which exist in the surface six inches of arable land may be thousands of millions.

Though the majority of nematodes lay eggs, some are viviparous; and the habits of the different species vary considerably. Their enormous numbers, almost universal location and greatly varying habits make them the most important of the parasites which materially affect the welfare of the human race. Though only a single worm may, in some instances, be found in one host, there are occasions when the numbers present are quite fantastic. In one case on record 25,000 were found in a lamb. They may occur in the intestines of their hosts or encysted in the flesh, in which case they are often in their larval form.

An encysted nematode

DISEASES AND PARASITES OF FRESHWATER FISH
Proboscis Worms   by H. S. Joyce

THE scientific name of Proboscis Worms, *Acanthocephala*, is derived from two Greek words, *acantha*, a spine and *kephale*, a head. They are irregularly shaped and their heads are armed with hooks. No examples of these creatures have been found possessing either a digestive system, a mouth, a circulatory or an excretory system. It is therefore evident that they live entirely by absorbing food which has been prepared previously by their hosts. Most of the Proboscis Worms are small and rarely attain a length of more than a few millimetres. Some of them are parasitic on birds, some on mammals and quite a number on fish. Very little is known about their life-histories. The larva uses an insect or small crustacean as a host, and the adult develops and lives in the digestive system of either a bird, mammal, or fish which swallows it in the larval state. Those found in freshwater fish are usually from larvae which inhabited freshwater shrimps.

One form, *Echinorhynchus proteus*, has been found in its young state in gudgeon, trout and pike. As time passes they bury their proboscis and neck in the wall of the intestines; and in this condition appear as a small orange-coloured knob. In the case of old trout and large pike they may grow to an inch in length. The larval form of this species is sometimes found in the liver of a minnow and develops to the adult state when the minnow is swallowed by a predatory fish.

Among the numerous species which affect freshwater fish, many of which bear a close outward resemblance, *E. clavula* is found in trout, bream and common carp; *E. angustatus* occurs in perch, pike and barbel; and *E. truttae*, usually spoken of as hookworm, is common to both ducks and trout. Trout which are badly infected often become blackish and lose their ability to change colour under the influence of light. They are in fact one of the causes for black trout. Unless this parasite is present in unusual numbers, it does not appear to affect a fish beyond the alteration in its colour and the elimination of its ability to change colour in response to its surroundings and the lighting conditions in which it lives.

E. nodulosus, another form which affects trout, is a relatively large creature, i.e. about a quarter-of-an-inch in length. There are a number of other varieties and it is probable that every species of freshwater fish is subject to

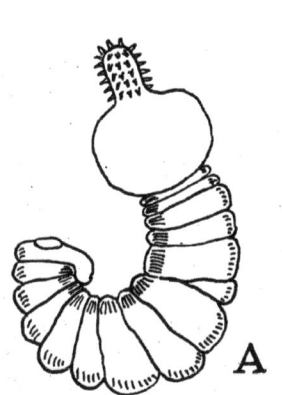
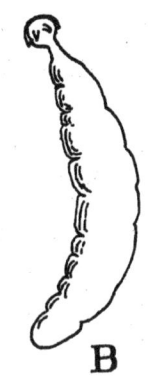
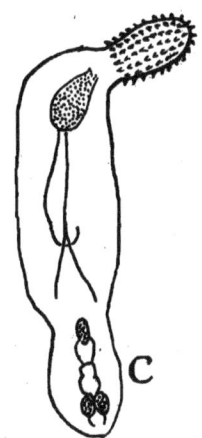

Proboscis Worms
A. *Echinorhynchus nodulosus.* B. *E. augustatus.* C. *E. truttae*

attack from one or other of them. An authority states that almost every perch, chub, carp, barbel, bream and roach examined was found to carry these parasites in its intestines.

One variety of Proboscis Worm which closely resembles *E. truttae* is very common in seafish; but, strangely perhaps, it is never found in either salmon or sea-trout. Salmon smolts and parr seem also to be immune from attack by any of the many species of these worms.

DISEASES AND PARASITES OF FRESHWATER FISH
Hag-fish and Lampreys by H. S. Joyce

THOUGH hag-fish are salt-water parasites, I have included them in this series of articles because they habitually attack salmon. They do, of course, prey on other fish and cod are among their most frequent victims.

The hag-fish is a blind, eel-like hermaphrodite, the mouth of which, though lipless, is furnished with four sensitive feelers. It occurs most frequently on the East coast; but, in spite of accounts which create the impression that it is, a common enemy of salmon, it is in fact quite rare and the majority of salmon-netsmen have never seen one.

This parasite has several popular names, of which borer, slime eel and glutinous hag are the most common. "Slime eel" and "glutinous" hag result no doubt from the quantities of slime which the creature secretes when taken from the water. A single hag is capable of filling a two-gallon bucket with slime and water in a few seconds and will repeat the performance after a short interval. Hag-fish attack their prey by boring into it, and then feed upon it steadily until only bone and skin remain.

There are four species of lamprey in this country: the sea lamprey, the river lampern, the pride or mud lamprey, and planer's lamprey. The last two, though very similar in habit, are slightly different in size and appearance. Some authorities regard these as varieties of the same fish, which differ in size because of their varying modes of life. Sea lampreys spend most of their life in the sea, and come into the rivers only to spawn. The lampern and planer's lamprey, which are intermediate in size, spend only a short time in the sea; and the pride, which is the smallest, never enters sea water.

All these creatures are boneless: their skeleton is cartilaginous, and their spine is a rudimentary form of vertebrae column or notochord.

Sea lampreys are very common in the North Atlantic and are more frequently seen in West coast rivers and in Ireland than on the East coast. They were much more common in times past than they are today: the decrease in their numbers is attributed to the almost universal pollution of our estuaries.

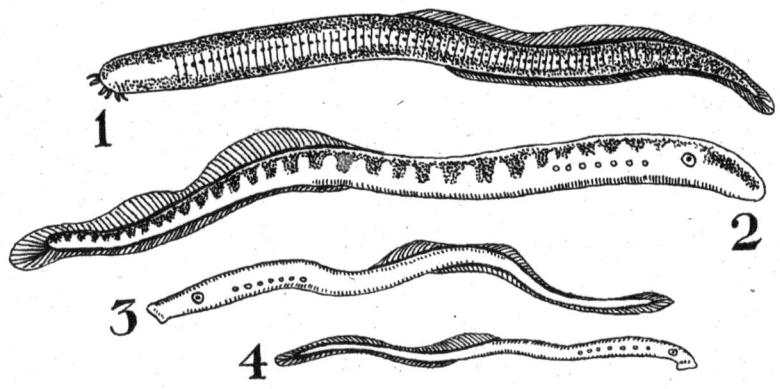

1. Hagfish. 2. Sea lamprey. 3. River lampern. 4. Mud lampern

They spawn as a rule in the lower waters of rivers, between February and June, after which they drift downstream in a comatose condition and in most cases die before they regain the sea. They attach themselves to their host (fish) and feed by rasping away the flesh with their tongue.

River lamperns are considerably smaller, rarely exceeding sixteen inches in length, and ascend rivers to spawn in April and May. They are sometimes seen on gravelly shallows, tugging at stones to form a trench for their eggs, and are probably more dangerous to fish than sea lampreys, because of their habit of boring right into their prey.

There was at one time a lamprey-fishery on the Severn, and the city of Gloucester was obliged to send a dish of lampreys (lamperns) to the King on his accession and each year at Christmas. On one occasion during the reign of King John this service was overlooked or neglected and the angry monarch fined the city forty marks.

Henry I is said to have eaten so many potted lampreys that the surfeit caused his death. That lampreys fried make a very tasty dish I can vouch, and I can imagine that anyone of gluttonous tendencies might well take too many of them. As a boy I usually managed to secure one dish a year; but I could never get more than a dozen at a time, as I had to catch them by hand. None of the other members of my family would ever touch "the horrid things", though, rather inconsistently I thought, they were always ready for a dish of fried eels.

The mud lampern, or pride, spends the whole of its life in fresh water, hibernates in the mud during the winter and is seen in the daytime only during the spawning season in April or May. It is said not to attack fish, a statement which is, I think, supported by the fact that it is often used as bait.

Planer's lamprey, which resembles the river lampern in outward structure, is much smaller; and, though it may be no longer than a mud lampern, is very much thicker. Mud lamperns are exceedingly slender little fish. Some authorities claim that planer's lampreys do occasionally go to sea; but, so far as I can discover, there is no record of their attacking other fish.

www.ingramcontent.com/pod-product-compliance
Ingram Content Group UK Ltd.
Pitfield, Milton Keynes, MK11 3LW, UK
UKHW041422180426
11947UKWH00007B/238